Biblical Reprobation

A primer on the most hated and neglected doctrine

SONNY L. HERNANDEZ

χάρις ὑμῖν καὶ εἰρήνη ἀπὸ Θεοῦ πατρὸς ἡμῶν
καὶ Κυρίου Ἰησοῦ Χριστοῦ.

For His Glory!

Special thanks to "Villie," Larry, and Angelina for encouraging me to write this concise primer on biblical reprobation.

TABLE OF CONTENTS

FOREWORD

The summation of Scripture is God's priority, which is His glory. Believers should keep God's glory in the forefront of their renewed minds. This would eliminate the glory of man, even expose it, so the renewed mind, by faith, can squash it.

God's Word teaches that all believers grow in the grace and knowledge of the Lord Jesus Christ, whom God has effectually called. We know God almighty, in His wisdom, has predestinated the use of means to grow His children as they read His infallible, inspired Word, hear solid biblical preaching and teaching, and are led by the Spirit into all truth.

The elect of God have heard the voice of the True Shepherd. This is the One who laid down His life exclusively for His sheep (John 10:11). Christ told the others, "But ye believe not, because ye are not of my sheep, as I said unto you" (John 10:26). Thus, eternal election and reprobation were clearly taught in John 10.

Praise the Lord that salvation is of the Lord from start to finish! The heart of the gospel points to the person and work of Christ, who infallibly secured the salvation of the elect, and He established perfect righteousness. Christ's righteousness will be effectually imputed to His people in each generation for their justification.

Lectures on God's eternal love and hatred have been perverted in pulpits today, which are antithetical to the testimony of Scripture. Many attempts have been made to chisel down sovereign grace doctrines in various aspects, which grow increasingly obvious as time goes on.

The compromise of God's sovereign grace has been a problem throughout history with people following the doctrines or traditions of men. The offense of sound doctrine is the last thing most professing Christians want to be identified with. As a result, doctrines such as unconditional election and reprobation are blatantly ignored.

The continual compromise among the Calvinist and Reformed circles, so to speak, is one reason a book like this is needed. It's time to get back to Scripture alone as the ultimate authority instead of opinions, secular philosophy, traditions, or even confessions of faith.

What typically happens when gospel teachers take an uncompromising stance on the biblical doctrine of predestination? There will be many accusations. This book will clearly teach what the Word of God says in its context, and it will show Christians how to refute slanderous accusations like hyper Calvinism, etc.

Men who deny reprobation will typically say, "Be careful what you blame God for," "Supralapsarianism is intellectual rhetoric we have no business talking about," "This doctrine is a mystery," and "The secret things belong to the Lord." And the list goes on and on.

The resistance to sound doctrine is transparent. When men deny reprobation, they will try to get God *off the hook*, so to speak, for His absolute sovereignty. They will also apologize to people for the doctrine of reprobation, or they will simply avoid it.

Biblical clarity has been suppressed for way too long. The call for God's people to boldly and unashamedly stand for the glory of God's free and sovereign grace in Christ should be our goal. When doing so, we also see God's glory is shown in the salvation of the elect, but also seen in the reprobation of the wicked.

What should the subject of reprobation cause in our attitude? God's people are made to see their place under their Master and to honor His glorious character. These believers are also shown in Scripture how to respond to others. The doctrine of sovereign election and reprobation will humble believers, and these saints will embrace God's sovereign purpose in election with reverence and godly fear.

Believers should always remember the mercy and grace they have been shown by God, in Christ. Therefore, when teaching and discussing doctrines, believers should show mercy, love, patience, care, and compassion to others.

Our prayer is to grow more. It seems clear that believers grow and mature in humility. This book will help us get a better understanding of the doctrine of reprobation from the Scripture. May the Lord bless His Word as it is taught in truth, in its context, for His glory.

Scott Price
Pastor, Gospel of Grace Ministries

CHAPTER 1
THE OFFENSE OF ELECTION/REPROBATION

The Bible undeniably teaches the Father's sovereign election, the Son's particular and plenteous redemption, and the Spirit's irresistible and effectual calling of the elect of God for whom Christ died. This is factual, and cannot be refuted.

Put another way, the Father chose the elect for salvation (Romans 8:29-30), not reprobate, the Son died for the sheep (John 10:11, 15), not goats, and the Spirit seals the invisible church (Ephesians 1:13), not those outside of it. This demonstrates perfect unity in the operation of the Godhead.

Paul, an ardent predestinarian, was not ashamed to preach on God's sovereign plan of election or particular grace because he was committed to the whole counsel of God (Acts 20:27). Similarly, a Christian herald will teach all of the truths contained in Scripture.

But a compromiser or hireling will not. Instead, when a compromiser or hireling sees a biblical text on sovereign election, particular grace, or limited atonement, he will intentionally remove the offense of sovereign election or the offense of the cross in their teachings.

For example, moderate Calvinists, also known as crypto Arminians, will say they believe in the doctrines of sovereign grace, yet many are surreptitious about these truths or they will intentionally use inclusive language.

Moderates will claim to be Calvinists, but many will avoid using the words elect, reprobation, or particular redemption. How do they do this? Instead of saying, "Christ died for the elect," moderates will say, "Christ died for all who would believe" because they know it's less offensive or it mitigates the offense.

Basically, moderate Calvinists will claim to believe in the doctrines of grace, but many will intentionally or deliberately remove the offense found in these truths. The following examples will explain how crypto Arminians will omit the offense of sovereign election and the cross from the doctrines of grace.

I. Compromisers and hirelings will remove the offense of sovereign election and the offense of the cross.

a. *Total depravity*

The Bible teaches the doctrine of total depravity. This means all men without exception are born into this world desperately wicked *as can be* because Adam sinned against God, and thereby incurred upon himself and all of humanity the penalty of sin and death (Romans 5:12).

Nonetheless, since total depravity is offensive to many, moderate Calvinists or crypto Arminians will remove the offense of this doctrine by saying, "The biblical view of total depravity does not mean men are *as bad as they can be*."

However, Genesis 6:5 does not say God saw that the wickedness of man was *not as bad as it can be*; instead, this text states, "And God saw that **the wickedness of man was great in the earth**, and that **every imagination of the thoughts of his heart was only evil continually**" (emphasis mine).

Additionally, Jeremiah 17:9 doesn't say the heart is *not as deceitful as it can* be; on the contrary, this text states, "**The heart is**

deceitful above all things, and desperately wicked: who can know it" (emphasis mine)?

b. *Unconditional election*

The Bible teaches that God actively chose His particular people, namely the elect, on the basis of His free and immutable will, and to the praise of His glorious grace (Ephesians 1:4-6). In fact, the apostle's underlying point in Romans 8:29-30 was to demonstrate that God's inviolable plan of sovereign election could never be thwarted. This text states,

> [29] For whom he did foreknow, he also did predestinate to be conformed to the image of his Son, that he might be the firstborn among many brethren. [30] Moreover whom he did predestinate, them he also called: and whom he called, them he also justified: and whom he justified, them he also glorified.

Moderate Calvinists will claim to believe in unconditional election, but many will intentionally omit the offense of God's sovereign election by saying, "Yes, God chose only the elect, but He desires to save even the non-elect, and thus gives a well-meant offer of salvation to even those who will never be saved."

The so-called well-meant offer of salvation doctrine teaches that God loves and desires to save all men, and thus offers salvation to even those whom the Father never decreed to save, which can be confirmed by reading Murray and Stonehouse's "Report of the Committee on the Free Offer of the Gospel."

It's ironic that the well-meant offer doctrine—championed by Murray and Stonehouse—is similar to what the heretic Billy Graham taught at his revivals. Therefore, the well-meant offer doctrine is basically the moderate Calvinist version of the Arminian altar call. This is one reason why moderate Calvinists are referred to as crypto Arminians.

c. *Particular redemption*

According to John 10, Jesus died exclusively for the sheep (v. 11), and He told the false teachers they were not His sheep (v. 26). Therefore, Christ did not die for all men because all men are not His sheep.

Since particular redemption is offensive to Arminians, moderate Calvinists will remove the offense of the cross, and say, "Christ died for the sheep in John 10:11, but His death was sufficient for all men." This argument is intentionally stupefying for the following reasons:

- The Bible does not teach that Christ's death is sufficient for all men without exception.

- Christ's blood is not sufficient for all because He did not die for all without exception.

- Asserting that Christ's death was sufficient for all is a hypothetical theory, not a biblical fact; thus, Christians embrace what the Bible teaches, not hypothetical or theoretical notions.

- Arguing that Christ died for the elect, but His blood was sufficient for all, is a subtle way compromising Calvinists will remove the offense of the cross, and simultaneously affirm Calvinism (*particular* redemption) and Arminianism (Christ's death is sufficient for *all*).

d. *Irresistible grace*

In Romans 8:30, Paul taught on God's eternal purpose, effectual calling, and the doctrine of justification. This text states, "Moreover whom he did predestinate, them he also called: and whom he called, them he also justified: and whom he justified, them he also glorified."

Paul's use of the demonstrative pronoun "them" (toutous, τούτους) indicates that those whom the Father decreed to save would undeniably be called, justified and glorified (οὓς δὲ προώρισε, **τούτους** καὶ ἐκάλεσε, καὶ οὓς ἐκάλεσε, **τούτους** καὶ ἐδικαίωσεν, οὓς δὲ ἐδικαίωσε, **τούτους** καὶ ἐδόξασε, emphasis mine). This means God's grace is irresistible, and no one or thing could ever stifle His inviolable plan of election.

According to the Bible, God's grace is always irresistible, efficacious, immutable and discriminative—and it is only applied to the elect. Put another way, when the context of Scripture specifically refers to *God's grace* [Hebrew: noun חֵן (ḥēn); verb חָנַן (ḥānan); Greek: noun χάρις (charis); verb χαρίζομαι (charizomai)], it is only applied to the elect [source of justification (Romans 3:24), and post conversion (2 Corinthians 12:9-10)], and never to the reprobate.

But since moderate Calvinists are compromisers, they will remove the offense of God's discriminative grace by saying, "God's grace is irresistible for only some, but He also gives common grace to all men, including the reprobate."

Put another way, moderates believe God gives common grace to the non-elect, but the Bible never says God's grace is common, and the Word of God teaches that God's grace is only given to the elect, not reprobate. This is why the moderate Calvinist doctrine of common grace, which is a myth, should be regarded as compromising, not Christian.

e. *Perseverance of the saints*

The Bible teaches that the elect of God for whom Christ died will be sealed by the Spirit. Christ stated in John 10:28, "And I give unto them eternal life; and they shall never perish, neither shall any man pluck them out of my hand."

In the Greek New Testament (NT), there is a double negative followed by an aorist subjunctive in John 10:28 (κἀγὼ ζωὴν αἰώνιον δίδωμι αὐτοῖς, καὶ **οὐ μὴ ἀπόλωνται** εἰς τὸν αἰῶνα, καὶ οὐχ ἁρπάσει τις αὐτὰ ἐκ τῆς χειρός μου, emphasis mine), which indicates the following: …never ever [οὐ μὴ] + no possibility of perishing [ἀπόλωνται].

A notable Greek scholar named Daniel Wallace explained that the double negative + aorist subjunctive is the "strongest way to negate something in Greek" (Wallace, *Greek Grammar Beyond the Basics* (GGBB), 1996, p. 468).

In summary, John 10:28 indicates that the Triune God infallibly secured the salvation of the elect. But crypto Arminians will remove the offense of God's sovereign election and the cross by saying, "The saints will persevere, but God still desires to save even the non-elect, and He offers them salvation." This argument is heresy for the following reasons:

- The true gospel is a declaration of Christ's completed and saving work, not a well-meant offer.

- The Bible never says that God desires to save the non-elect, and it never says the gospel is an "offer."

- The Bible is patently clear that reprobates will never become elect, and goats will never become sheep.

- Put another way, according to the well-meant offer doctrine, God has an always failing desire to redeem the reprobate, but the Bible teaches that God accomplishes all that He desires (Isaiah 55:11).

- Therefore, it is impossible to faithfully teach on the biblical doctrine of reprobation and simultaneously affirm the unbiblical notion of the well-meant offer.

II. Compromisers and hirelings will avoid or grossly redefine the biblical doctrine of reprobation.

Since compromising Calvinists will remove the offense of sovereign election and the cross when teaching on the doctrines of grace, it should not be perplexing when they grossly redefine or avoid the biblical doctrine of reprobation.

Sadly, church members in a moderate Calvinist assembly would have a better chance of winning the lottery than they would seeing their pastor preach a full sermon on the biblical doctrine of reprobation or teach a sermon on God's unremitting hatred towards the reprobate or non-elect.

As a disclaimer, crypto Arminians will occasionally mention or reference reprobation and God's hatred. However, as stated earlier, they will be inclusive with the word reprobation, or they will grossly redefine the biblical doctrine of reprobation and God's hatred towards the non-elect.

According to Scripture, reprobation is defined in the following manner: in accordance with His free and immutable will and glory, God actively and unconditionally reprobated the wicked for hell (everlasting conscious torment), and thus has an unremitting hatred towards them, which can never be eradicated.

But since the biblical doctrine of reprobation and God's hatred is offensive to moderate Calvinists, they will try desperately to remove the offense of God's eternal purpose of election by positing one of the following *unbiblical* views:

- God actively chose the elect for salvation, but He only passively reprobated the wicked, meaning He only permitted, allowed, or let reprobation take place.

- God reprobated the wicked because He foresaw in eternity who would reject Him.

- God reprobated the wicked because they rejected Him.

- Reprobates harden themselves because God allowed it.

- God passively reprobated the wicked, but desires to redeem reprobates, loves reprobates, gives common grace to reprobates, and offers salvation to reprobates.

- God hated Esau in Romans 9:13, but the word *hate* means to *love less*, or God simultaneously loved and hated Esau.

As shown above, since the biblical doctrine of reprobation is offensive to compromising Calvinists, they will grossly redefine this doctrine to remove the offense, and they will label men as hyper

Calvinists if they disagree with their crypto Arminian interpretation of the doctrine of reprobation.

Interestingly, Arminians will also accuse Calvinists of being hyper Calvinists when they teach on the doctrines of grace. This is why it's not surprising when crypto Arminians accuse sovereign grace believers of being hyper Calvinists.

For the record, this book does not advocate for hyper Calvinism, but condemns it. Hyper Calvinists restrict the preaching of the gospel, and they will not preach Christ to all men, but only to some they think are elect. This view is heresy. Instead, this book advocates for the following truths:

- Only the one true God who exists in a Trinity of persons knows who all of the elect and reprobate are (Romans 8:28-30; 9:10-24).

- Thus, God's Word commands Christians to preach Christ and Him crucified to all men promiscuously and indiscrimately (Mark 16:15).

III. Closing

Furthermore, the biblical doctrine of reprobation is the most hated and neglected doctrine, which lost people hate the most. Hirelings and compromisers will not preach on the biblical doctrine of reprobation, but Christian heralds will.

Biblical Reprobation is an important book for three reasons: (1) reprobation is a biblical doctrine (Romans 9:10-14); (2) gospel preachers believe and teach the whole counsel of God (Acts 20:27), (3) and the Lord takes glory for Himself, not just in the salvation of the elect (Revelation 4:11), but also in the reprobation of the wicked (Romans 9:17).

This book is an easy-to-read pamphlet and study guide on the the most hated and neglected doctrine (biblical reprobation), which are notes from a sermon preached at Trinity Gospel Church in Shelbyville, KY, on October 30, 2022.

For His Glory!

"For of him, and through him, and to him, are all things: to whom be glory for ever. Amen" (Romans 11:36).

CHAPTER 1 STUDY QUESTIONS

1. Explain how there is perfect unity in the operation of the Godhead.

2. What biblical text teaches that the Father chose the elect for salvation?

3. Does the Bible teach that Christ died for the elect or for everyone?

4. Moderate Calvinists are also known as what?

5. What kind of men are ashamed of teaching on sovereign election?

6. What is the doctrine of total depravity?

7. How do moderate Calvinists remove the offense of total depravity?

8. The apostle's underlying point in Romans 8:29-30 was to demonstrate what?

9. What is the well-meant offer?

10. The well-meant offer doctrine is basically the moderate Calvinist version of what?

11. What did Jesus tell the false teachers in John 10:26?

12. How do moderate Calvinists remove the offense of the cross when teaching on the atonement?

13. Why is it wrong to teach that Christ's death was sufficient for all?

14. Explain why common grace is unbiblical.

15. It is impossible to faithfully teach on the biblical doctrine of reprobation and simultaneously affirm the unbiblical notion of what?

16. Define the biblical doctrine of reprobation.

17. Explain some of the ways moderate Calvinists will redefine the biblical doctrine of reprobation.

18. Does Romans 9:13 teach that Esau was hated or loved less?

19. What is hyper Calvinism?

20. What biblical text adjures Christians to preach Christ and Him crucified to all men promiscuously and indiscriminately?

21. Who will not preach on the biblical doctrine of reprobation?

22. According to this chapter, what biblical doctrine is the most hated and neglected?

23. Explain in your own words why you agree or disagree with question 22.

24. Provide three reasons why the biblical doctrine of reprobation is important.

25. Would you talk about reprobation to an unbeliever?

CHAPTER 2
REPROBATION IS ACTIVE AND UNCONDITIONAL

When the biblical doctrine of reprobation is broached, moderate Calvinists will ashamedly say, "God chose the elect, then He passes over others," or they will say, "Reprobation is passive," meaning God only permits, allows, or lets it happen.

Since moderates know that it cannot be proven exegetically or linguistically that reprobation is passive, they will say, "paradox, mystery, antinomy, or we don't know," when pressed to exegetically defend their passive view.

However, the Bible provides a clear explanation on reprobation as active and unconditional, which will be discussed in this chapter. Before addressing several biblical texts, it's important to define, once again, the biblical doctrine of reprobation, and explain what is meant by active and unconditional.

According to the Bible, per His eternal and immutable will, and to the praise of His glory, God actively and unconditionally decreed or predestined the reprobate for hell (Romans 9:10-14). Therefore, God hates the reprobate (Psalm 5:5).

Active means God is the prime agent, or the sole ultimate cause of all things (Isaiah 46:10), who decreed, determined, ordained or predestined the goats to hell, also known as everlasting conscious torment.

The word unconditional emphasizes that God ordained or decreed the non-elect for hell, not on the basis of foreseen disbelief, but on the basis of His free and immutable will, and to the praise of His glorious grace (Romans 9:17, 20-22).

Additionally, since this chapter will address a few texts in Romans, it's important to remember that Arminians think Paul's epistle has nothing to do with the individual salvation of God's elect. This aforementioned argument is easy to refute because the apostle provided several singular indications.

Examine the following singular words in Romans 9, which refute the Arminian notion that this chapter is not dealing with the individual salvation of God's elect.

> **v. 15**: For he saith to Moses, I will have mercy on *whom* I will have mercy, and I will have compassion on *whom* I will have compassion.

> τῷ γὰρ Μωϋσῇ λέγει· ἐλεήσω **ὃν** ἂν ἐλεῶ, καὶ οἰκτειρήσω **ὃν** ἂν οἰκτείρω (emphasis mine).

> **v. 16**: So then it is not of him that *willeth*, nor of him that *runneth*, but of God that sheweth mercy.

> ἄρα οὖν οὐ τοῦ **θέλοντος** οὐδὲ τοῦ **τρέχοντος**, ἀλλὰ τοῦ ἐλεοῦντος Θεοῦ (emphasis mine).

> **v. 17**: For the scripture saith unto Pharaoh, Even for this same purpose have I raised *thee* up, that I might shew my power in *thee*, and that my name might be declared throughout all the earth.

> λέγει γὰρ ἡ γραφὴ τῷ Φαραὼ ὅτι εἰς αὐτὸ τοῦτο ἐξήγειρά **σε**, ὅπως ἐνδείξωμαι ἐν **σοὶ** τὴν δύναμίν μου, καὶ ὅπως διαγγελῇ τὸ ὄνομά μου ἐν πάσῃ τῇ γῇ (emphasis mine).

> **v. 18**: Therefore hath he mercy on *whom* he will have mercy, and *whom* he will he hardeneth.

ἄρα οὖν ὃν θέλει ἐλεεῖ, **ὃν** δὲ θέλει σκληρύνει (emphasis mine).

v. 20: Nay but, O ***man***, who art thou that repliest against God? Shall the ***thing*** formed say to him that formed it, Why hast thou made me thus?

μενοῦνγε, ὦ **ἄνθρωπε**, σὺ τίς εἶ ὁ ἀνταποκρινόμενος τῷ Θεῷ; μὴ ἐρεῖ τὸ **πλάσμα** τῷ πλάσαντι, τί με ἐποίησας οὕτως (emphasis mine);

As shown above, the use of the singular words demonstrates that God's eternal purpose deals with the individual salvation of the elect, and the reprobation of the wicked. This chapter will now examine a few biblical texts to demonstrate that reprobation is active and unconditional.

I. Romans 9:10-13

[10] And not only this; but when Rebecca also had conceived by one, even by our father Isaac; [11] (For the children being not yet born, neither having done any good or evil, that the purpose of God according to election might stand, not of works, but of him that calleth;) [12] It was said unto her, The elder shall serve the younger. [13] As it is written, Jacob have I loved, but Esau have I hated.

After reading Romans 9:10-13, one can easily deduce that the moderate Calvinist or crypto Arminian interpretation of the doctrine of reprobation is imbecilic and unbiblical. Examine the following reasons why.

Moderates have long argued that God actively chose the elect, but only passively (permits or allows) reprobated the wicked to hell. But Romans 9 says, "…the purpose of God according to election might stand" (v. 11), and "…but of him that calleth" (Ibid.). This indicates that God is the one who actively and unconditionally chose Jacob, and actively and unconditionally reprobated Esau.

Moderates and many Arminians think God reprobated the wicked because He foresaw in eternity who would reject Him. Yet, Romans 9:11 refutes this Arminian notion. This text states, "(For the children being not yet born, neither having done any good or evil, that the purpose of God according to election might stand, not of works, but of him that calleth)."

Moderates and Arminians have also argued that God reprobated the wicked because they rejected Him. But Romans 9, once again, refutes moderate Calvinism and Arminianism when it says, "not yet born," "neither having done any good or evil," and "not of works" (Ibid.).

Moreover, many moderates and Arminians will argue that reprobates harden themselves because God allows it. Romans 9:11 does not say "the purpose of *men* according to what God *allows* might stand," and it does not say "but of him that *allows* it."

God is eternal and immutable, and His purpose is eternal and immutable; therefore, the eternal and immutable purpose of the almighty God does not depend on men's decisions, but the Master's decree.

Furthermore, some moderates will teach that God passively reprobated the wicked, but desires to redeem reprobates, loves reprobates, gives common grace to reprobates, and offers salvation to reprobates.

However, the context of Romans 9, which deals with the salvation of the elect and the reprobation of the wicked, says nothing about God's love for goats or desire to save reprobates, and it certainly never promotes the doctrine of *common* grace because it is nothing more than a myth or an Arminian invention.

Bottom line: Romans 9:10-13 proves God actively and unconditionally predestined Jacob, and thus loves him. This text also proves God actively and unconditionally reprobated Esau, and thus has an unremitting hatred towards him.

II. Romans 9:22

What if God, willing to shew his wrath, and to make his power known, endured with much longsuffering the vessels of wrath fitted to destruction.

εἰ δὲ θέλων ὁ Θεὸς ἐνδείξασθαι τὴν ὀργὴν καὶ γνωρίσαι τὸ δυνατὸν αὐτοῦ ἤνεγκεν ἐν πολλῇ μακροθυμίᾳ σκεύη ὀργῆς κατηρτισμένα εἰς ἀπώλειαν.

As shown above, Romans 9:22 does not say "vessels of wrath God *allowed* to be fitted to destruction," and it does not say, "vessels of wrath that fitted *themselves* to destruction." There is no passive language (permits, allows, or lets happen) in this text.

The perfect tense verb *prepared* or *fitted* (katartizō, κατηρτισμένα) is in the passive voice. This grammatically rules out the idea that God only permitted reprobates to be fitted to destruction, and it certainly doesn't imply that God fitted the vessels of wrath to destruction because of foreseen disbelief.

Prepared or fitted (katartizō, κατηρτισμένα) indicates that the vessels of wrath were eternally fitted to destruction by God. Scholars have argued that κατηρτισμένα means "**of men whose souls God has so constituted** that they cannot escape destruction" (Thayer, *Thayer's Greek-English Lexicon of the New Testament*, 2019 [1896], p. 336), or "…designed for destruction" (BDAG, 2000, p. 526).

III. Matthew 15:12-14

[12] Then came his disciples, and said unto him, Knowest thou that the Pharisees were offended, after they heard this saying? [13] But he answered and said, Every plant, which my heavenly Father hath not planted, shall be rooted up. [14] Let them alone: they be blind leaders of the blind. And if the blind lead the blind, both shall fall into the ditch.

After Christ, God the Logos, rebuked the Pharisees for their hypocrisy, the disciples informed Him that the false teachers were offended. The response Christ gave was a clear indication of the biblical doctrine of reprobation. Matthew 15:13 states:

…**Every plant, which my heavenly Father hath not planted, shall be rooted up** (emphasis mine).

Per the context of Matthew 15:13, the words *plant* or *planted* undeniably refer to the biblical doctrine of election due to the fact Christ said "every plant" (v. 13), after being told the Pharisees were offended (v. 12).

Put another way, the words *plant* and *planted* come after Christ was informed the Pharisees were offended (v. 12), and they are immediately followed by Christ's statement, "Let **them** (masculine) alone: **they be** (third person) blind leaders of the blind…" (v. 14, emphasis).

Some may object to "every plant" referring to the biblical doctrine of election, but those who object are ignoring context, or they fail to understand that plants don't plant themselves, just like babies don't choose their parents when they are born.

The plants that were planted by the Father point to the sheep or children of God, and the plants that were not planted by the Father refer to the sons of perdition, the begotten of the pit, or the children of the devil, namely the reprobate. Therefore, the plants that were uprooted by the Father refer to the vessels of wrath fitted to destruction or the reprobate.

Also, it's important to note that Jesus never said, "Every plant, which my heavenly Father hath not planted, shall be *allowed or permitted* to be rooted up." He also never mentioned anything about offering salvation to reprobates, or giving them common grace and benevolence; instead, Christ preached on the biblical doctrine election in v. 13, and subsequently said in v. 14:

> Let them alone: they be blind leaders of the blind. And if the blind lead the blind, both shall fall into the ditch.

IV. John 10:26

> But ye believe not, because ye are not of my sheep, as I said unto you.

John 10:26 is another text that teaches the biblical doctrine of reprobation. There are a few points that need to be addressed in this passage.

- Christ did not assert that the false teachers were not His sheep *because* they rejected the well-meant offer of salvation.

- Christ did not say the false teachers were not His sheep *because* they chose not to believe in the gospel.

- Christ never gave a disclaimer to the false teachers that they are still His *brothers* even though they do not believe in the doctrine of particular redemption, which He taught in vv. 11, 15.

Christ told the false teachers that they did not believe because they are "not my sheep," which indicates they were reprobates. Biblically, men who are not the sheep of Christ are referred to as goats, i.e., reprobates. See Matthew 25:31-33:

> [31] When the Son of man shall come in his glory, and all the holy angels with him, then shall he sit upon the throne of his glory: [32] And before him shall be gathered all nations: and he shall separate them one from another, **as a shepherd divideth his sheep from the goats**: [33] **And he shall set the sheep on his right hand, but the goats on the left** (emphasis mine).

The whole context of John 10 proves v. 26 is referring to reprobation. For example, before Christ told the false teachers that they are not His sheep, He told those who are *not His sheep* that they do not believe what He says (v. 25), but subsequently said *the sheep* "hear" and "follow" Him (v. 27).

It is important to compare Christ's words in John 10:27 ["I know them" (sheep)] with Matthew 7:23 ["I never knew you" (reprobate)].

According to John 10, Christ died for "the sheep" (vv. 11, 15), Christ "**knows**" the sheep" (v. 27, emphasis mine), the Father gave Christ the sheep (v. 29), and Christ promises eternal life to the sheep (vv. 28-29). This is a testimony of true love.

But in Matthew 7:23, Christ said, "**I never knew you**" (emphasis mine), which indicates the exact opposite of John 10: The Father never gave the goats to Christ, the Savior never died for the goats, and the goats are never promised eternal life. This is a testimony of God's hatred towards the reprobate.

V. Closing

Thus far, it has been shown that reprobation is a biblical doctrine, and it is active and unconditional, not passive. The Bible says nothing about God permitting, allowing, or letting reprobation take place, and it never implies reprobation is a mystery or paradox.

So when moderate Calvinists affirm passive reprobation, meaning God allows or permits the reprobation of the wicked, they need to be asked, "If God only allows or permits the reprobation of the wicked, then who is the ultimate cause of reprobating the wicked?" This question is important.

Arguing that God permits, allows, or lets reprobation happen presupposes that there is a metaphysical power or force in the universe that competes with God or that can cause something to come to pass outside of the will or decree of God (See Cheung, *The Author of Sin*, 2014). This form of dualism is heresy, and it must be rejected.

God is the sole ultimate cause of everything, meaning He literally determined everything, and the Bible makes it patently clear that nothing takes place outside of the eternal purpose and immutable will of God.

As the prime agent, God decreed, determined, or ordained all things (Isaiah 46:10), including the "…wicked for the day of evil" (Proverbs 16:4), and He works all things after the counsel of His will (Ephesians 1:11). This includes every word men speak, nothing excluded.

> **Lamentations 3:37-39**: Who is he that saith, and it cometh to pass, when the Lord commandeth it not? Out of the mouth of the most High proceedeth not evil and good? Wherefore doth a living man complain, a man for the punishment of his sins?

> **Proverbs 21:1**: The king's heart is in the hand of the LORD, as the rivers of water: he turneth it whithersoever he will.

Therefore, God actively and unconditionally predestined the elect for heaven, and He actively and unconditionally predestined the wicked for hell. God loves the former (elect), and hates the latter (reprobated).

For His Glory!

CHAPTER 2 STUDY QUESTIONS

1. What do moderate Calvinists say when the doctrine of reprobation is broached?

2. Define the biblical doctrine of reprobation.

3. What biblical text teaches that God hates?

4. What do active and unconditional mean?

5. Why is the doctrine of reprobation so offensive to many people?

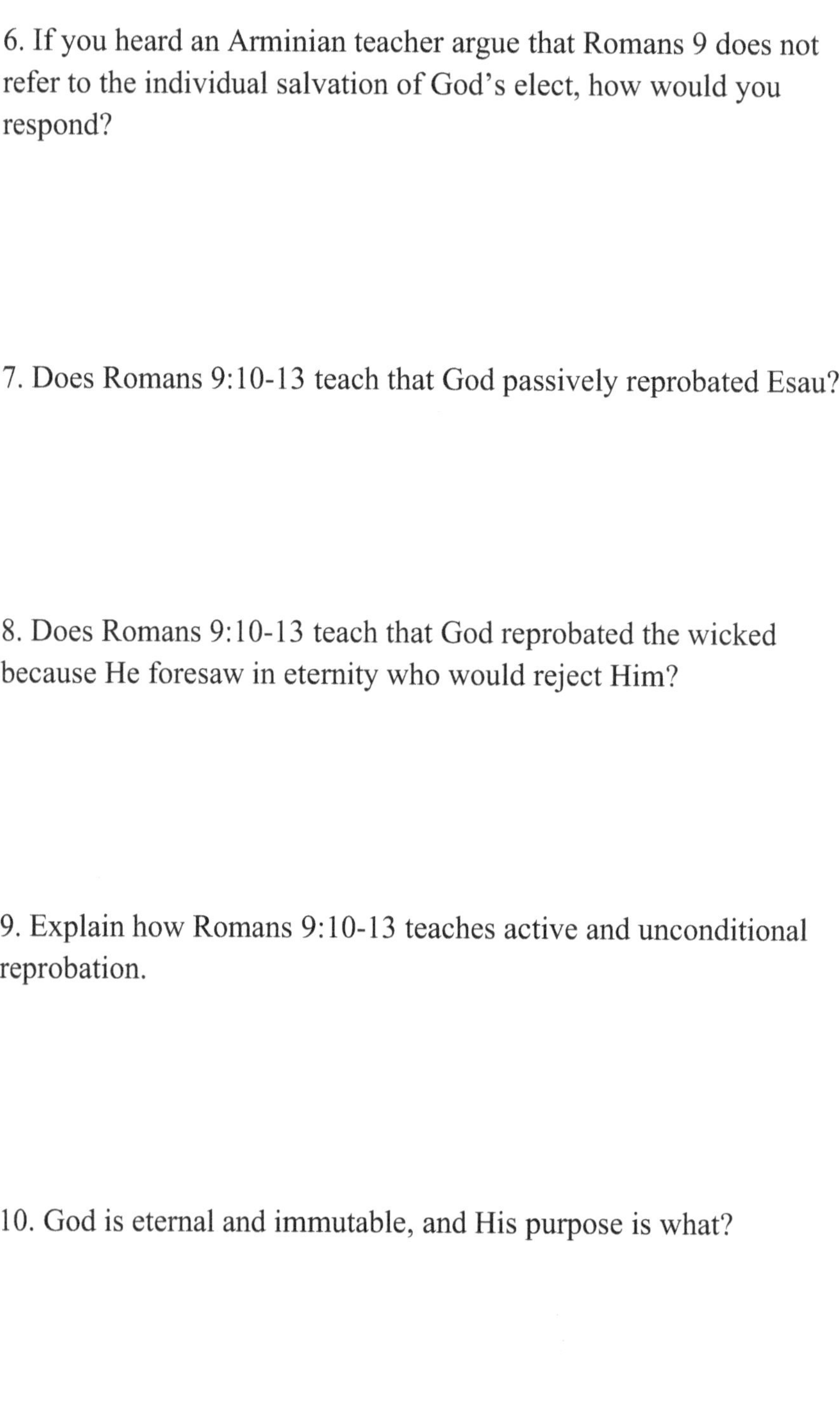

6. If you heard an Arminian teacher argue that Romans 9 does not refer to the individual salvation of God's elect, how would you respond?

7. Does Romans 9:10-13 teach that God passively reprobated Esau?

8. Does Romans 9:10-13 teach that God reprobated the wicked because He foresaw in eternity who would reject Him?

9. Explain how Romans 9:10-13 teaches active and unconditional reprobation.

10. God is eternal and immutable, and His purpose is what?

11. The eternal and immutable purpose of the almighty God does not depend on what?

12. Is there any passive language in Romans 9:22?

13. The word *prepared* or *fitted* in Romans 9:22 indicates what?

14. Explain how Matthew 15:13 teaches the biblical doctrine of reprobation.

15. Per the context of Matthew 15:13, the words *plant* or *planted* undeniably refer to the biblical doctrine of what?

16. Some may object to "every plant" (Matthew 15:13) referring to the biblical doctrine of election, but those who object are ignoring what?

17. The plants that were uprooted by the Father in Matthew 15:13 refer to what?

18. Explain why John 10:26 teaches the doctrine of reprobation.

19. In John 10:26, did Jesus say, "You are not my sheep because you chose not to believe"?

20. Explain why it is important to compare Christ's words in John 10:27 ["I know them" (sheep)] with Matthew 7:23 ["I never knew you" (reprobate)].

21. If a moderate Calvinist tells you that he affirms passive reprobation, meaning God allows or permits the reprobation of the wicked, what important question should you ask him?

22. Arguing that God permits, allows, or lets reprobation happen presupposes what?

23. Who is the sole ultimate cause of everything?

24. Nothing takes place outside of what?

25. Who does God hate?

CHAPTER 3
REPROBATION AND GOD'S UNREMITTING HATRED TOWARDS THE NON-ELECT

The doctrine of reprobation is biblical, and it teaches the following: in accordance with His free and immutable will, and to the praise of His glorious grace, God actively and unconditionally predestined the wicked to hell, and has an unremitting hatred towards them.

According to Scripture, God does not desire to save reprobates, God does not love reprobates, God does not give grace to reprobates, and God never offers salvation to reprobates. This chapter will provide several reasons why.

I. God does not provide a well-meant offer of salvation to reprobates.

Contextually, Romans 9:10-13 undeniably teaches that God actively and unconditionally reprobated Esau, and it also teaches that Esau was hated by God, not loved. In fact, nowhere in Scripture does it teach that God desired to save Esau; nor does it say that God loved Esau in any sense, and it certainly never maintains that God offered salvation to Esau.

As a result, moderate Calvinists cannot and will not faithfully teach on the biblical doctrine of reprobation. This is because many of them affirm the so-called well-meant offer doctrine, which can be summarized by examining the *conclusions* to Murray and Stonehouse's "Report on the Committee on the Free Offer of the Gospel."

(1) We have found that the grace of God bestowed in his ordinary providence expresses the love of God, **and that this**

love of God is the source of the gifts bestowed upon and enjoyed by the ungodly as well as the godly…

(2) **We have found that God himself expresses an ardent desire for the fulfilment of certain things which he has not decreed in his inscrutable counsel to come to pass**. This means that there is a will to the realization of what he has not decretively willed, a pleasure towards that which he has not been pleased to decree…

(3) Our Lord himself in the exercise of his messianic prerogative provides us with an example of the foregoing as it applies to the matter of salvation. **He says expressly that he willed the bestowal of his saving and protecting grace upon those whom neither the Father nor he decreed thus to save and protect**.

(4) …This will of God to repentance and salvation is universalized and reveals to us, therefore, **that there is in God a benevolent lovingkindness towards the repentance and salvation of even those whom he has not decreed to save**. This pleasure, will, desire is expressed in the universal call to repentance.

(5) We must conclude, therefore, that our provisional inference on the basis of Matt. 5:44–48 is borne out by the other passages. **The full and free offer of the gospel is a grace bestowed upon all**… (emphasis mine; see Orthodox Presbyterian Church's website to examine the entire report that was presented to the Fifteenth (1948) General Assembly of the Orthodox Presbyterian Church—SLH).

After examining the excerpts above, it can easily be deduced that Murray and Stonehouse believed the following: God's common

grace and love are given to everyone, God desires to save all men
without exception, and God provides a well-meant offer of salvation
to even those whom He has not decreed to save, i.e., the non-elect.

The doctrine of reprobation is biblical, whereas the well-meant offer is not. In fact, both doctrines are diametrically opposed, which is why moderates and Arminians deny the biblical definition of reprobation.

There are some who try to simultaneously hold to the biblical doctrine of reprobation and the unbiblical doctrine of the well-meant offer, but embracing this stance is compromising, not Christian. Review the following points:

- The well-meant offer teaches that God loves everyone, but the Bible teaches that God only loves the elect (Romans 5:5; Ephesians 5:25), and hates the non-elect (Psalm 5:5).

- The well-meant offer teaches that God desires to save all men, yet all men will not be saved (Matthew 7:13-14; Revelation 20:11-15). But the Bible teaches that God accomplishes all that He desires (Isaiah 55:11).

- The well-meant offer teaches that God gives common grace to the non-elect, but the Bible teaches that *God's grace* is only applied to the elect [source of justification (Romans 3:24), and post conversion (2 Corinthians 12:9-10)], and never to the non-elect.

- The well-meant offer teaches that God, in the internal call, offers the gospel to even those whom He has not decreed to save, but the Bible never says the gospel is "offered."

- The Bible never says the gospel is offered or proffered to men, but says, "**For the preaching of the cross is to them that perish foolishness**; but unto us which are saved it is the power of God" (1 Corinthians 1:18, emphasis mine).

- Jesus never offered salvation to the false teachers, but told them, "…I never knew you: **depart from me**, **ye that work iniquity**" (Matthew 7:23, emphasis mine).

- However, Mark 16:15 *does* teach that Christians are to preach Christ to all men (external call), without exception. Nonetheless, preaching the gospel means Christ's completed and saving work is proclaimed, not offered.

II. God does not love reprobates.

The Bible does not teach that God loves all men, but Arminians maintain that God loves everyone. So it's no surprise that moderate Calvinists, also known as crypto Arminians, will also assert that God's benevolence or love is also given to the non-elect. Examine the following texts to see that God does not love all men:

Psalm 5:5: The foolish shall not stand in thy sight: thou hatest all workers of iniquity.

Psalm 11:5-6: [5] The LORD trieth the righteous: but the wicked and him that loveth violence his soul hateth. [6] Upon the wicked he shall rain snares, fire and brimstone, and an horrible tempest: this shall be the portion of their cup.

Romans 9:13: As it is written, Jacob have I loved, but Esau have I hated.

Instead of embracing the biblical texts above, which clearly teach that God does in fact hate certain men, many Arminians will say, "God loves the sinner, but hates the sin," and moderates will either ignore biblical texts like Psalm 5:5, or say that hate means "love less," or "God simultaneously loves and hates the non-elect."

However, arguing that "God hates the sin but loves the sinner" is absurd because the Bible does not support this aforementioned assertion. And the Bible is clear that sinners are cast into hell, not doctrines.

Additionally, Romans 9:13 does not say that Esau was "loved less," but hated, and it certainly does not indicate that Esau was simultaneously loved and hated by God. This text explicitly says, "…Jacob have I loved, but Esau have I hated."

As a disclaimer, the Bible doesn't teach that God loves the non-elect; it states that God "…**hatest all workers of iniquity**" (Psalm 5:5, emphasis mine). And the Word of God never teaches that God hated the elect; Scripture teaches that God eternally loved the elect before the creation of the world (Ephesians 1:3-6).

Since moderate Calvinists and Arminians believe God loves everyone, and doesn't hate the non-elect, they will twist John 3:16, and argue that it teaches God's love for the whole world. This passage states:

For God so loved the world, that he gave his only begotten Son, that whosoever believeth in him should not perish, but have everlasting life.

οὕτω γὰρ ἠγάπησεν ὁ Θεὸς τὸν κόσμον, ὥστε τὸν υἱὸν αὐτοῦ τὸν μονογενῆ ἔδωκεν, ἵνα πᾶς ὁ πιστεύων εἰς αὐτὸν μὴ ἀπόληται, ἀλλ' ἔχῃ ζωὴν αἰώνιον.

John 3:16 does not teach God's universal love for every single person who has ever lived in the world. Yes, this text starts by saying, "For God so loved the world…," but *world* does not always refer to each and every single person. Context must determine how *world* is interpreted.

Arminians and many moderate Calvinists think the use of the word *world* in John 3:16 teaches God's universal love, but that can be refuted since Jesus said He did not pray for the "world," but only for those whom the Father gave to Him (John 17:9). Christ also said that His disciples were "not of the world," and are hated by the world (John 15:18-19).

Thus far, it has been shown that the word *world* does not always refer to each and every single person. What is the *world* referring to in John 3:16? According to the context, the *world* in John 3:16 is referring to those who are presently believing.

Yes, the King James Version says "whosoever," but this word is not in the Greek NT (John 3:16). The English word *whosoever* is a pronoun, but the Greek word uses the word $\pi\tilde{\alpha}\varsigma$, which is an adjective ("all").

Also, the word "believe" in the KJV is a present active participle. This means the word "believe" in the KJV must be interpreted as *believing*. Therefore, examine the literal translation for John 3:16:

> for [conj. ἵνα] all [adj. πᾶς] the [art. ὁ] believing [part. πιστεύων] in [conj. εἰς] Him [Jesus] should not perish but have everlasting life.

So, those "believing in Him" cannot be referring to reprobates because goats do not and will never believe. Remember, in John 10:26, Christ told the false teachers, **"But ye believe not, because ye are not of my sheep**, as I said unto you" (emphasis mine).

In summary, John 3:16 teaches that God loves the elect in the world who are believing in Christ. Some may object to Christ only loving the elect, not all men. Thus, examine the following illustration, which presents biblical truth:

A faithful husband professes love only for his bride, not all women. Similarly, Jesus, the faithful high priest (Hebrews 2:17), only loves His bride, the church, or elect for whom He died (Ephesians 5:25).

Additionally, a godly man will not commit adultery because he loves his bride. Likewise, the God-Man, Christ Jesus, will not commit adultery either because He loves His bride, i.e., the elect (Romans 8:33-39).

III. **God does not give common grace to reprobates**.

God does not give common grace to anyone for the simple fact that the Bible never says God's grace is "common." And the Bible never teaches that God gives grace, favor, love, or mercy to reprobates.

Since moderate Calvinists and Arminians know the Bible never says God's grace is "common" and never teaches that God's grace is given to the non-elect, they will appeal to Matthew 5:45. This text states:

That ye may be the children of your Father which is in heaven: **for he maketh his sun to rise on the evil and on**

the good, and sendeth rain on the just and on the unjust (emphasis mine).

Interestingly, moderates think Matthew 5:45 teaches that God gives common grace or non-salvific love to even the non-elect, but this passage doesn't even mention the word grace or love, and it doesn't say God "maketh his *common grace* to rise on the evil…," or, "He sendeth *non-salvific love* on the unjust."

Since the Bible never explicitly says that God's grace or love is ever applied to the non-elect or reprobate, moderates think the rising of the sun and the sending of rain are evidence that God gives common grace or love to reprobates.

Well, if the rising of the sun and the sending of rain, per moderates, proves God gives non-salvific grace or love to the non-elect, do thunderstorms or tornadoes mean God hates them also? Absolutely not.

The rising of the sun and the sending of rain does not refer to the common grace myth, but to God's providence because He "…worketh all things after the counsel of his own will" (Ephesians 1:11).

Instead of appealing to weather to determine who God gives grace or love to, true Christians appeal to the Bible because it explicitly teaches the following:

God's grace: The elect, not reprobate, are saved by grace alone (source of justification), and the grace of God is always applied to the sheep (post conversion), not goats. Romans 3:24 states, "Being justified freely by his grace…," and 2 Corinthians 12:9 states, "… My grace is sufficient for thee."

God's love: God loves the elect, and hates the reprobate. See the following evidence: "…the love of God is shed abroad in our (elect) hearts" (Romans 5:5), and God "…hatest all workers of iniquity" (Psalm 5:5).

Also, compromisers will appeal to superstition when they say, "Given the fact that God does not immediately send reprobates to hell is proof He gives them common grace or has a non-salvific love for them."

But Christians appeal to Scripture to determine why God does not immediately send the goats or reprobates to hell. For example, in Psalm 73, the psalmist saw the wicked had "prosperity" (v. 3), "strength" (v. 4), "more than heart could wish" (v. 7), and "riches" (v. 12).

Since God did not immediately send the wicked to hell, did the psalmist experience God's common grace? Absolutely not! According to vv. 18-20, the psalmist witnessed the wicked being fattened for destruction:

> [18] Surely **thou didst set them in slippery places**: **thou castedst them down into dest**ruction. [19] How are they **brought into desolation**, as in a moment! **they are utterly consumed with terrors**. [20] As a dream when one awaketh; so, O Lord, when thou awakest, **thou shalt despise their image** (emphasis mine).

In Psalm 92:7, does it say, "When the wicked spring as the grass, and when all the workers of iniquity do flourish; it is that *God has prolonged hell so they could experience His common grace*"? No! This text states, "…the wicked spring as the grass, and when all the workers of iniquity do flourish; **it is that they shall be destroyed for ever**" (emphasis mine).

When moderates say, "Since God does not immediately send the wicked to hell, it's proof He gives common grace to the non-elect," they are making it known that they are either ignorant of Jeremiah 12:3 or have ignored this passage.

According to Jeremiah 12:3, God prolongs judgment on the wicked because He is fattening them for the day of slaughter. This text states, "…**pull them out like sheep for the slaughter, and prepare them for the day of slaughter**" (emphasis mine).

Lastly, James 5:5 is another example why it's asinine to say, "Since God does not immediately send the wicked to hell, it's proof He gives common grace to the non-elect." This text states, "Ye have lived in pleasure on the earth, and been wanton; **ye have nourished your hearts, as in a day of slaughter**" (emphasis mine).

Note: for an in-depth examination and refutation of common grace and the well-meant offer, see Sonny Hernandez, *A Rebuttal of Common Grace and the Well-Meant Offer* (2021), which is available on Amazon (kindle and paperback).

IV. Closing

This chapter has demonstrated the following truths: according to the Bible, God does not love the wicked, He does not give grace to the non-elect, He does not desire to save reprobates, and He does not offer salvation to those whom He has not decreed to save.

Since God actively and unconditionally predestined the goats to hell, He only desires their damnation, and prolongs their final judgment to fatten them for the day of destruction, per His eternal purpose and immutable will.

Bottom line: Christ never told the wicked He loved them; nor did He extend grace to them, and He never offered salvation to reprobates, but said the following:

- "…I never knew you: depart from me, ye that work iniquity" (Matthew 7:23).

- "Ye are of your father the devil…" (John 8:44).

- "…ye are not of God" (John 8:47).

- "But ye believe not, because ye are not of my sheep…" (John 10:26).

- "…I pray not for the world (non-elect), but for them which thou hast given me; for they are thine" (John 17:9).

Christ made the aforementioned statements because the elect or sheep were predestined to heaven and the reprobates or goats were predestined to hell. Therefore, God loves the elect, and has an unremitting hatred towards the wicked. This is why Romans 9:13 states, "As it is written, Jacob have I loved, **but Esau have I hated**" (emphasis mine).

For His Glory!

CHAPTER 3 STUDY QUESTIONS

1. The doctrine of reprobation is biblical, and it teaches what?

2. Since God actively and unconditionally reprobated the wicked, He hates whom?

3. What biblical text undeniably teaches that God actively and unconditionally reprobated Esau?

4. Does the Bible teach or imply that God desired to save Esau?

5. The so-called well-meant offer is popularly held by whom?

6. How come moderate Calvinists will not present a faithful exposition of the biblical doctrine of reprobation?

7. The doctrine of reprobation is biblical, whereas the well-meant offer is what?

8. The well-meant offer teaches that God loves everyone, but the Bible teaches what?

9. God's grace is only applied to whom?

10. Does the Bible ever say the gospel is "offered"?

11. What does 1 Corinthians 1:18 teach?

12. Mark 16:15 *does* teach that Christians are to preach Christ to whom?

13. Does the Bible teach that God loves all men?

14. What does Psalm 5:5 teach?

15. How do moderate Calvinists interpret Psalm 5:5?

16. Arguing that "God hates the sin but loves the sinner" is what?

17. Since moderate Calvinists and Arminians believe God loves everyone, and doesn't hate the non-elect, they will twist what biblical text?

18. Does John 3:16 teach God's universal love for every single person who has ever lived in the world?

19. What biblical text teaches that Christ did not pray for the world?

20. In summary, John 3:16 teaches that God loves whom?

21. Does God give common grace to all men?

22. The rising of the sun and the sending of rain in Matthew 5:45 does not refer to the common grace myth, but to what?

23. Since God did not immediately send the wicked to hell in Psalm 73, did the psalmist experience God's common grace?

24. According to Jeremiah 12:3, why did God prolong judgment on the wicked?

25. Did Christ teach common grace or the well-meant offer in Matthew 7:23?

CHAPTER 4
REPROBATION AND ELECTION ARE EQUALLY ULTIMATE IN THE DECREE OF GOD

Moderate Calvinists have long argued that God only actively and unconditionally chose the elect, and the ones not chosen (reprobates) refer to those whom the Father had *passed by* or *left* to themselves. This compromising approach is meant to mitigate or remove the offense of election.

Additionally, moderate Calvinists and Arminians will either deny the biblical doctrine of double predestination, or they will teach that election and reprobation are not equally ultimate in the decree of God.

This chapter will present a consistent supralapsarian approach to defend the following biblical truths: election and reprobation are equally ultimate in the decree of God, and denying the biblical doctrine of reprobation is tantamount to rejecting the biblical doctrine of predestination, i.e., God's sovereign plan of election.

I. Concise overview of supralapsarianism

The supralapsarianism versus infralapsarianism debate has taken place for many years. Since many have no idea what these terms mean, it's important to provide a concise definition of supralapsarianism and infralapsarianism.

The debate between supralapsarianism versus infralapsarianism is also known as the *logical order* of decrees, and it focuses on predestination, creation, and the fall.

Put another way, did God decree the salvation of the elect *before* He ordained creation and the fall? Or, did God decree the salvation of the elect *after* He ordained creation and the fall. A supralapsarian would say "yes" to the former, whereas, an infralapsarian would say "yes" to the latter.

Thus, supra (before) + lapsarianism (the fall) teaches that God decreed the salvation of the elect *before* He ordained creation and the fall, and infra (after) + lapsarianism (the fall) maintains that God decreed the salvation of the elect *after* He ordained creation and the fall.

But the most important part of the supralapsarianism versus infralapsarianism discussion is and will always be Christ—God the Logos—which is often overlooked. Since Christ is in every way God, but distinct from the Father, He conceived, created, and controls all things.

Therefore, Christ must be first in the supralapsarianism versus infralapsarianism discussion, which most infralapsarians will not agree with. Examine the following biblical text (Colossians 1:16):

> For by him were all things created, that are in heaven, and that are in earth, visible and invisible, whether they be thrones, or dominions, or principalities, or powers: all things were created by him, and for him:

> ὅτι ἐν αὐτῷ ἐκτίσθη τὰ πάντα, τὰ ἐν τοῖς οὐρανοῖς καὶ τὰ ἐπὶ τῆς γῆς, τὰ ὁρατὰ καὶ τὰ ἀόρατα, εἴτε θρόνοι εἴτε κυριότητες εἴτε ἀρχαὶ εἴτε ἐξουσίαι·τὰ πάντα δι' αὐτοῦ καὶ εἰς αὐτὸν ἔκτισται·

In the text above, there are three significant prepositional phrases or grammatical constructions that need to be examined: preposition (ἐν) + dative (αὐτῷ), preposition (δι') + genitive (αὐτοῦ), preposition (εἰς) + accusative (αὐτὸν).

First, the preposition (ἐν) + dative (αὐτῷ) or "by him" means Christ is the chief architect, and nothing takes place outside of His detailed plan.

For example, in the planning or building phase, an architect cannot facilitate or effectively lead a team without detailed blueprints. Similarly, nothing takes place outside of the mind of Christ. This is why Colossians 1:16 states:

> **For by him were all things created**, that are in heaven, and that are in earth, visible and invisible, whether they be thrones, or dominions, or principalities, or powers… (emphasis mine).

Second, the preposition (δι') + genitive (αὐτοῦ) or "by him" in Colossians 1:16 is also seen in John 1:3, which states, "All things were made **by him** [preposition (δι') + genitive (αὐτοῦ)]; and without him was not any thing made that was made" (emphasis mine).

Grammatically, when the context refers to the person of Christ, who is wholly God (distinct from the Father) and wholly man (without sin), the preposition (δι') + genitive (αὐτοῦ) indicates ultimate agency. This means Christ is the ultimate agent of creation.

Third, the last prepositional phrase does not indicate that Christ carried out the act for the Father, but for Himself. Colossians 1:16 states, "…all things were created by him, and **for him** [preposition (εἰς) + accusative (αὐτὸν), emphasis mine].

In summary, the three prepositional phrases [preposition (ἐν) + dative (αὐτῷ), preposition (δι') + genitive (αὐτοῦ), preposition (εἰς) + accusative (αὐτὸν)] can easily be called the "three c's," which means Christ *conceived*, *created*, and *controls* all things. Therefore, Christ comes first in the logical order of decrees.

Moreover, in the supralapsarianism versus infralapsarianism debate or discussion about theological determinism and the superstitious notion of free will, one question always seems to come up: Where did the sin come from that caused Adam to fall?

Infralapsarians, moderate Calvinists, and Arminians will typically respond to the question by saying, "We don't know," or "No one knows." These responses are troubling for the following reasons.

The Bible is clear that nothing takes place outside of the will or decree of God (Isaiah 46:10; Ephesians 1:11). Many will object to this because they think it's wrong to argue that God ordained evil, but the Bible never says or even implies that God ordaining sin is a sin.

According to Scripture, God does as He pleases (Psalm 115:3; 135:6), and sin is only attributed to created beings, not the Creator. Thus, God ordained all things, including the sin that caused Adam to fall.

> **Proverbs 16:4**: The LORD hath made all things for himself: yea, ***even the wicked for the day of evil*** (emphasis mine).

> **Isaiah 45:7**: I form the light, and create darkness: I make peace, ***and create evil***: I the LORD do all these things (emphasis mine).

Acts 2:23 is an important text, which also demonstrates that Christ comes first in the logical order of the supralapsarianism versus infralapsarianism discussion. This passage also proves that it's absurd to argue that no one knows where the sin comes from that caused Adam to sin. Acts 2:23 states:

> Him, being delivered by the determinate counsel and foreknowledge of God, ye have taken, and by wicked hands have crucified and slain.

> τοῦτον τῇ ὡρισμένῃ βουλῇ καὶ προγνώσει τοῦ Θεοῦ ἔκδοτον λαβόντες, διὰ χειρῶν ἀνόμων προσπήξαντες ἀνείλετε·

In the text above, it's important to note that both nouns, *βουλῇ* ("counsel") and *προγνώσει* ("foreknowledge"), are in the dative case, and both nouns are connected by the conjunction *καὶ* ("and"). *βουλῇ* is articular [has definite article; lit., *the* determined counsel], whereas *προγνώσει* is anarthrous (without definite article).

According to the Granville Sharp Rule (see Wallace, *GGBB*, 1996, p. 270-290), the grammatical construction above [def. art. ("the) + noun (dat. "counsel") + conj. ("and") + noun (dat. "foreknowledge")] indicates that the latter noun ("foreknowledge") is a farther description of the first ("counsel"). This means, per the immutable will of God, the substitutionary and particular death of Christ was decreed in eternity.

Therefore, when men say, "We don't know where the sin came from that caused Adam to fall," they need to be asked the following question, "Are you saying that God got lucky when Adam ate from that forbidden fruit?"

If moderates say "no" to the aforementioned question above, they are conceding, admittedly or not, that God did decree Adam's sin. Or, if moderates say, "God only permitted the fall," meaning God is not the ultimate cause of the fall, which indicates that someone or something can cause something to come to pass outside of the decree of God. This heresy is called dualism.

However, if moderates say "no," this implies the following: according to moderate Calvinists, if Adam had chosen not to sin, God would be a liar for determining or ordaining the death of Christ (Acts 2:23). Romans 3:4 states, "God forbid: yea, let God be true, but every man a liar…"

In 2 Samuel 24:10, David was grieved because he sinned against God, and He said to the Lord, "…**I have sinned greatly in that I have done**: and now, I beseech thee, O LORD, take away the iniquity of thy servant; for I have done very foolishly" (emphasis mine). But what cannot be overlooked is the fact that God is the one who caused Adam to sin in 2 Samuel 24:1:

> And again the anger of the LORD was kindled against Israel, **and he moved David against them to say, Go, number Israel and Judah** (emphasis mine).

Similarly, Adam sinned against God, and it was the Lord who ordained Adam to transgress His law. Bottom line: Acts 2:23 proves that God ordained the substitutionary death of the Son, and 2 Samuel 24:10 indicates that men are responsible for the sin they commit. But God is the sole ultimate cause of all things, including David's sin (2 Samuel 24:1). This is because God does as He pleases (Psalm 115:3).

Therefore, in the logical order, God ordained the substitutionary and particular death of the Son (Acts 2:23; Colossians 1:16), then He predestined the salvation of the elect and the reprobation of the wicked (Romans 9:13, 21) *before* He decreed creation and the fall (Genesis 1-3). This was done in accordance with His free and immutable will, and to the praise of His glorious grace.

II. A closer look at equal ultimacy

In confessional circles, so to speak, the doctrine of equal ultimacy is either met with ire or confusion because many people use several definitions for this doctrine. This section of the chapter will explain how equal ultimacy is explained by moderates, and how this chapter defines this doctrine.

First, many Calvinists believe equal ultimacy is synonymous with double predestination. The doctrine of double predestination simply means God predestined the elect to salvation, and He predestined the wicked to hell.

Since many Calvinists, not all, reject double predestination, they will also deny equal ultimacy, and affirm the following: single predestination, passive reprobation, or they will argue that reprobation only takes place when men reject God, and they will appeal to Judas or Romans 1:28.

Romans 9 does not teach single predestination, and it does not say or even imply that reprobation is passive. Review the following biblical texts:

Romans 9:10-13: [10] And not only this; but when Rebecca also had conceived by one, even by our father Isaac; [11] (For the children being not yet born, neither having done any good or evil, that the purpose of God according to election might stand, not of works, but of him that calleth;) [12] It was said unto her, The elder shall serve the younger. [13] As it is written, Jacob have I loved, but Esau have I hated.

Romans 9:17-18: [17] For the scripture saith unto Pharaoh, Even for this same purpose have I raised thee up, that I might shew my power in thee, and that my name might be declared throughout all the earth. [18] Therefore hath he mercy on whom he will have mercy, and whom he will he hardeneth.

Romans 9:21-23: [21] Hath not the potter power over the clay, of the same lump to make one vessel unto honour, and another unto dishonour? [22] What if God, willing to shew his wrath, and to make his power known, endured with much longsuffering the vessels of wrath fitted to destruction: [23] And that he might make known the riches of his glory on the vessels of mercy, which he had afore prepared unto glory.

As shown above, Romans 9:10-13 doesn't teach that God's purpose of election included Jacob, but *not Esau*. And it doesn't teach that God predestined Jacob, but only *passed by Esau*. Also, Romans 9:17 doesn't say, "Even for this same purpose have I *permitted* you to be raised up." And Romans 9:22 doesn't say the vessels of wrath "fitted *themselves* to destruction."

Basically, here is the point: passive language (God permitted, allowed, or let happen) and single predestination are doctrinal terms that come from Arminians and moderate Calvinists, not the infallible and inerrant Word of God.

In a desperate attempt to remove the offense of election, moderate Calvinists and Arminians will say, "Judas and Romans 1:28 prove God reprobated the wicked because they rejected Him," or they will say, "Judas is not in hell because God was the ultimate cause of His betrayal; instead, Judas is not in heaven because he chose to sin and rejected God."

The Bible clearly teaches that Judas betrayed Jesus (John 13:21-27). But to say that "Judas is not in hell because God was the ultimate cause of His betrayal" is ridiculous. Before Judas betrayed Christ, God's Word prophesied that Judas would be the one to betray the Master (Psalm 41:9; 55:12-14, 20-21; Zechariah 11:12-13).

Even before His death, Christ Jesus, God the Logos, said, "…but woe unto that man [Judas] by whom the Son of man is betrayed! it had been good for that man if he had not been born" (Matthew 26:24), and He referred to Judas as "a devil" (John 6:70).

Most notably, Jesus said, "While I was with them in the world, I kept them in thy name: those that thou gavest me I have kept, and none of them is lost, **but the son of perdition; that the scripture might be fulfilled**" (John 17:12, emphasis mine).

Similarly, when Romans 1:28 says the wicked "did not like to retain God in their knowledge, God gave them over to a reprobate mind…," moderates erroneously opine that God only reprobated the wicked because they rejected Him. This view explains secondary causes ("…**they** did not like to retain God in their knowledge," emphasis mine), but ignores the ultimate cause ("God").

According to the Bible, God created the wicked or reprobates for the day of evil (Proverbs 16:4); thus, the wicked or reprobates will undeniably reject God and act incorrigibly. First Peter 2:8 explains why: "…even to them which stumble at the word, being disobedient: **whereunto also they were appointed**" (emphasis mine).

Therefore, the wicked will in fact stumble and reject the Lord. That is because God decreed their reprobation. So the wicked will reject God in His appointed time, and God will give them over to a reprobate mind. Bottom line: God is the sole ultimate cause of all things, and men are responsible for their sins.

Second, moderate Calvinists will reject equal ultimacy because they believe it indicates the following:

- God equally creates a new heart in the elect and also a bad heart in reprobates.

- God equally works in the hearts of the elect to bring them to salvation as He does in the hearts of the non-elect to bring them to condemnation.

Yes, the Bible *does* teach that God creates a new heart in the elect (Ezekiel 36:25-27), but God doesn't need to create a bad heart in the reprobate because He decreed their perdition. As a result, goats are born into this world with stony hearts due to the fall (Genesis 3; Romans 5:12).

The Bible also teaches that God works in the hearts of the elect "…to will and to do of his good pleasure" (Philippians 2:13), and He ordained their works (Ephesians 2:10). But does the Bible teach that God works in the hearts of the non-elect? Yes. Examine the biblical texts below:

> **Deuteronomy 2:30**: But Sihon king of Heshbon would not let us pass by him: *for the LORD thy God hardened his spirit, and made his heart obstinate, that he might deliver him into thy hand*, as appeareth this day (emphasis mine).

> **Exodus 4:21**: And the LORD said unto Moses, When thou goest to return into Egypt, see that thou do all those wonders before Pharaoh, which I have put in thine hand: *but I will*

harden his heart, that he shall not let the people go
(emphasis mine).

Revelation 17:17: *For God hath put in their hearts to fulfil his will, and to agree, and give their kingdom unto the beast,* until the words of God shall be fulfilled (emphasis mine).

The texts above prove God *does* work in the hearts of the non-elect, but moderate Calvinists will insist that God actively causes the elect to believe, but He does not actively cause the non-elect to not believe.

Yet, God's Word explicitly teaches the following: David sinned against God, but it was God who caused David to sin. Christ spoke in parables because the wicked could not see or hear the truth. God is the one who blinded reprobates from seeing the truth, and He hardened their hearts so they could not understand and be converted. See the following biblical texts:

2 Samuel 24:1, 10: [1] And again the anger of the LORD was kindled against Israel, *and he moved David against them to say, Go, number Israel and Judah.* [10] And David's heart smote him after that he had numbered the people. *And David said unto the LORD, I have sinned greatly in that I have done*: and now, I beseech thee, O LORD, take away the iniquity of thy servant; for I have done very foolishly (emphasis mine).

Matthew 13:10-14: [10] And the disciples came, and said unto him, Why speakest thou unto them in parables? [11] He answered and said unto them, Because it is given unto you to know the mysteries of the kingdom of heaven, *but to them it is not given*. [12] For whosoever hath, to him shall be given, and he shall have more abundance: *but whosoever hath not, from him shall be taken away even that he hath.* [13] *Therefore speak I to them in parables: because they seeing see not; and hearing they hear not, neither do they understand.* [14] And in them is fulfilled the prophecy of Esaias, which saith, By hearing ye shall hear, and shall not understand; and seeing ye shall see, and shall not perceive (emphasis mine).

John 12:37-41: [37] But though he had done so many miracles before them, yet they believed not on him: [38] That the saying of Esaias the prophet might be fulfilled, which he spake, Lord, who hath believed our report? and to whom hath the arm of the Lord been revealed? [39] *Therefore they could not believe*, because that Esaias said again, [40] *He hath blinded their eyes, and hardened their heart; that they should not see with their eyes, nor understand with their heart, and be converted*, and I should heal them. [41] These things said Esaias, when he saw his glory, and spake of him (emphasis mine).

Third, what is a biblical definition for the doctrine of equal ultimacy? Equal ultimacy should be defined in the following manner: both election and reprobation are equally ultimate in the decree of God. Romans 9:11 states:

(For the children being not yet born, neither having done any good or evil, **that the purpose of God according to election might stand**, not of works, but of him that calleth)" (emphasis mine).

μήπω γὰρ γεννηθέντων μηδὲ πραξάντων τι ἀγαθὸν ἢ κακόν, ἵνα ἡ κατ᾽ ἐκλογὴν τοῦ Θεοῦ πρόθεσις μένῃ, οὐκ ἐξ ἔργων, ἀλλ᾽ ἐκ τοῦ καλοῦντος·

The noun πρόθεσις ("purpose") clearly refers to God's eternal, free, and immutable will. This is because Romans 9:11 states, "…the children being not yet born," "…neither having done any good or evil," and "…not of works, **but of him that calleth**" (emphasis mine).

It's also important to note that πρόθεσις in Romans 9:11 is singular, and His purpose includes the election of Jacob (God loved Jacob), and the reprobation of Esau (God hated Esau). This means election and reprobation are parts of predestination, and election and reprobation refer to the same decree, not separate ones.

A simple word study of πρόθεσις in the NT will demonstrate that God's purpose is eternal, free, immutable, and absolute:

Romans 8:28: And we know that all things work together for good to them that love God, to them who are the called according to his *purpose* (emphasis mine).

Ephesians 1:11: In whom also we have obtained an inheritance, being predestinated according to the *purpose* of him who worketh all things after the counsel of his own will (emphasis mine).

Ephesians 3:11: According to the eternal *purpose* which he purposed in Christ Jesus our Lord (emphasis mine).

2 Timothy 1:9: Who hath saved us, and called us with an holy calling, not according to our works, but according to his own *purpose* and grace, which was given us in Christ Jesus before the world began (emphasis mine).

Another notable text, which teaches that election and reprobation are parts of predestination, and are equally ultimate in the decree of God is Romans 9:21. This text states:

> Hath not the potter power over the clay, **of the same lump** to make one vessel unto honour, and another unto dishonor" (emphasis mine)?

> ἢ οὐκ ἔχει ἐξουσίαν ὁ κεραμεὺς τοῦ πηλοῦ, ἐκ τοῦ αὐτοῦ φυράματος ποιῆσαι ὃ μὲν εἰς τιμὴν σκεῦος, ὃ δὲ εἰς ἀτιμίαν·

The same lump ("φυράματος") is singular, and the image of the potter and clay signify the following: in the eternal decree (singular) of God, He predestined the elect ("vessel unto honour"), and He reprobated the goats (vessels "unto dishonor").

John Gill's commentary on Romans 9:21 is worth reading because it emphasized that God is glorified in the salvation of the elect ("vessel unto honour"), and the reprobation of the wicked (vessels "unto dishonor"):

> …with respect to the vessels of honour, whom he appoints for his glory, he determines to create them; to suffer them to fall into sin, whereby they become polluted and guilty; to raise and recover them, by the obedience, sufferings, and death of his Son; to regenerate, renew, and sanctify them, by his Spirit and grace, and to bring them to eternal happiness; and hereby compass the aforesaid end, his own glory, the glorifying of his grace and mercy, in a way consistent with justice and holiness: with respect to the vessels of dishonour, whom he also appoints for the glorifying of himself, he determines to create them out of the same lump; to suffer them to fall into sin; to leave them in their sins, in the pollution and guilt of them, and to condemn them for them;

and hereby gain his ultimate end, his own glory, glorifying
the perfections of his power, justice, and holiness, without
the least blemish to his goodness and mercy: now if a potter
has power, for his own advantage and secular interest, to
make out of the same clay what vessels he pleases; much
more has God a power, out of the same mass and lump of
creatureship, to appoint creatures he determines to make to
his own glory; which he brings about by different methods,
consistent with the perfections of his nature (Gill, *Romans
9:21*, 2006 [1809], p. 510-511).

III. Closing

This chapter has presented a consistent supralapsarian
approach to defend a biblical view of equal ultimacy. This doctrine
is certainly not popular among moderate Calvinists, but the Bible
teaches that Christians seek to please God, not men (Galatians 1:10).

Since election and reprobation are parts of predestination,
and election and reprobation refer to the same decree, rejecting or
ignoring reprobation is tantamount to rejecting and ignoring the
biblical doctrine of election.

According to Ephesians 1, the doctrine of predestination is in
accordance with "…the good pleasure of his will" (v. 5). In this
chapter, Paul also explained the goal of election, and he said, "To the
praise of the glory of his grace…" (v. 6).

Therefore, the so-called pastors who will not preach on
reprobation are in fact not teaching the biblical doctrine of election,
which robs God of His glory. May God have mercy on whom He
wills, and "…whom he will he hardeneth" (Romans 9:18).

For His Glory!

CHAPTER 4 STUDY QUESTIONS

1. What compromising approach is meant to mitigate or remove the offense of election?

2. The debate between supralapsarianism versus infralapsarianism is also known as what?

3. What does supralapsarianism teach?

4. What does infralapsarianism teach?

5. The most important part of the supralapsarianism versus infralapsarianism discussion is and will always be whom or what?

6. Why is Colossians 1:16 an important biblical text?

7. The Bible is clear that nothing takes place outside of what?

8. The Bible never says or even implies that God ordaining sin is what?

9. Is the Granville Sharp Rule easy to understand?

10. What is dualism?

11. Does 2 Samuel 24:10 teach that David sinned?

12. Who caused David to sin (see 2 Samuel 24:1)?

13. In confessional circles, so to speak, the doctrine of equal ultimacy is met with what?

14. What is double predestination?

15. Does Romans 9 teach single predestination?

16. Passive language (God permitted, allowed, or let happen) and single predestination are doctrinal terms that come from whom?

17. According to the Bible, God created the wicked or reprobates for the day of what?

18. What biblical text says, "…whereunto also they were appointed?"

19. Does the Bible teach that God works in the hearts of the non-elect?

20. Does the Bible teach that God is the one who blinded reprobates from seeing the truth?

21. What is a biblical definition for the doctrine of equal ultimacy?

22. What biblical text teaches that election and reprobation are parts of predestination, and are equally ultimate in the decree of God?

23. What doctrine is certainly not popular among moderate Calvinists?

24. Rejecting or ignoring reprobation is tantamount to rejecting and ignoring the biblical doctrine of what?

25. What is the goal of election?

CHAPTER 5
CONCLUSION: REPROBATION IS FOR GOD'S GLORY

The biblical doctrine of reprobation is often overlooked, ignored, or misinterpreted. Instead of ignoring or overlooking reprobation, Christians need to carefully examine this biblical doctrine, and they will see how many theologians and pastors have grossly redefined the doctrine of reprobation.

Many theologians and pastors will not preach on reprobation because they don't feel it is edifying to tell Christians or unbelievers that God chose some for perdition and thus hates them. And moderate Calvinists will not teach on reprobation because it stands in opposition to the well-meant offer.

Nonetheless, the doctrine of reprobation must be preached because it is a biblical doctrine and it gives God glory. Therefore, if a so-called pastor does not preach on the doctrine of reprobation, he is abdicating his responsibility to preach the whole counsel of God, and is robbing God of glory.

This chapter will provide a few biblical reasons why the doctrine of reprobation must not be silenced, ignored, twisted, or maligned. These biblical texts will help Christians respond to common objections to reprobation, and they will also help believers understand why it's important to study this doctrine.

I. God is just in the reprobation of sinners.

Romans 9:20-21: [20] Nay but, O man, who art thou that repliest against God? Shall the thing formed say to him that formed it, Why hast thou made me thus? [21] Hath not the

potter power over the clay, of the same lump to make one
vessel unto honour, and another unto dishonour?

II. God is glorified in the reprobation of sinners.

Romans 9:17: For the scripture saith unto Pharaoh, Even for
this same purpose have I raised thee up, that I might shew my
power in thee, and that my name might be declared
throughout all the earth.

Revelation 4:11: Thou art worthy, O Lord, to receive glory
and honour and power: for thou hast created all things, and
for thy pleasure they are and were created.

III. God displays His love for the elect in the reprobation of sinners.

Romans 9:22-23: [22] What if God, willing to shew his wrath,
and to make his power known, endured with much
longsuffering the vessels of wrath fitted to destruction: [23] And
that he might make known the riches of his glory on the
vessels of mercy, which he had afore prepared unto glory,

IV. God does as He pleases in the reprobation of sinners.

Romans 9:15, 18: [15] For he saith to Moses, I will have mercy
on whom I will have mercy, and I will have compassion on
whom I will have compassion. [18] Therefore hath he mercy on
whom he will have mercy, and whom he will he hardeneth.

V. Closing

Additionally, the biblical doctrine of reprobation reminds
Christians that God is absolutely sovereign, and He does as He

pleases. Many will object to this, but it doesn't matter if men or women like it or not. God has and will always do as He pleases.

> **Deuteronomy 28:63**: And it shall come to pass, that as the LORD rejoiced over you to do you good, and to multiply you; so the LORD will rejoice over you to destroy you, and to bring you to nought; and ye shall be plucked from off the land whither thou goest to possess it.

> **1 Samuel 15:3**: Now go and smite Amalek, and utterly destroy all that they have, and spare them not; but slay both man and woman, infant and suckling, ox and sheep, camel and ass.

> **1 Kings 22:23**: Now therefore, behold, the LORD hath put a lying spirit in the mouth of all these thy prophets, and the LORD hath spoken evil concerning thee.

> **Psalm 105:25**: He turned their heart to hate his people, to deal subtilly with his servants.

> **Jeremiah 19:9**: And I will cause them to eat the flesh of their sons and the flesh of their daughters, and they shall eat every one the flesh of his friend in the siege and straitness, wherewith their enemies, and they that seek their lives, shall straiten them.

Bottom line: in accordance with His immutable will and divine sovereignty, God actively and unconditionally chose the elect, and He actively and unconditionally reprobated the wicked. God loves the former (elect), and hates the latter (reprobate). For His Glory!

APPENDIX A
THE PLACE OF REPROBATION IN THE PREACHING OF THE GOSPEL HERMAN HOEKSEMA (1886-1965)

The subject of this pamphlet is not an easy one,[1] but it is of great importance for those who love the Reformed truth. A Reformed person thinks and lives theologically. For him it is of greatest importance to know His God as He has revealed Himself in His works and Word. He understands perfectly that he cannot comprehend God, because God is infinite, His Being is unfathomable, and His works always fill us with adoring wonder. But still a Reformed man desires to know more and more about his God, and also to comprehend that which God has revealed of Himself.

God is One. There must therefore be unity in His revelation, unity of thought and purpose in all His works. And therefore a child of God, especially a Reformed child of God, cannot rest until he has learned to see and understand this unity of thought and purpose. It is from this point of view that we wish to consider the place of reprobation in the preaching of the Gospel.

We proceed, of course, in the discussion of this subject from the assumption that we are speaking to Reformed people. We shall not therefore speak now about election or reprobation as such. In fact, we shall not even make an attempt to defend the contention that reprobation should have a place in the preaching of the Gospel. We assume this. Rather, we shall attempt to trace the unity of God's

---

[1] Hoeksema, H. (n.d.). The Place of Reprobation in the Preaching of the Gospel. Protestant Reformed Churches in America Official Website. Retrieved November 9, 2022, from http://www.prca.org/pamphlets/pamphlet_50.html

works, and then place ourselves before this question: What is the place of reprobation in that unity?

We have said that we will consider the place of reprobation in the preaching of the Gospel. If reprobation must be preached, what is its place? How must it be presented? What is its relation to election and to the whole of truth; and with what emphasis must it be presented? It is obvious that in the preaching or instruction of the truth the various aspects of the truth must be placed in their proper light and in their relation to one another. If I should describe a masterpiece of an artist, and if I should attempt to describe the individual parts which are on the canvas without relating them to the whole, that masterpiece would be ruined by my description. Or if I should attempt to portray my impression of the whole and lay so much stress on the background that the background becomes the foreground, I do not do justice to the work of the artist. So it is also in respect to the work of salvation. One can very well, on occasion, preach on election, and later on reprobation, without setting forth these truths correctly, simply because he has not preached them in their mutual relation and in connection with the entire truth of Scripture.

The question is, therefore, What is the place of reprobation in the preaching of the Gospel? It lies in the nature of the case, however, that this question is inseparably connected with another, namely, What is the proper place of reprobation in the entire body of truth? Both election and reprobation are parts of predestination; and this again is part of the counsel of God in the full sense of the word as it pertains to all things. In order therefore to determine the place of reprobation in the works of God and in the preaching of the gospel, we must first of all review the whole plan of God concerning all things. Secondly, we must answer the question how predestination appears in this full counsel. And, finally, we must determine the relation in which reprobation stands to election, as far as this is possible in the light of Scripture.

We shall discuss all these things as we deal with: The Place of Reprobation in the Preaching of the Gospel.

I - God's Decree and Election

II - Election with Reprobation

III - Reprobation in the Preaching

God's Decree and Election

The question that confronts us is: What is the relation of election to God's decree concerning all things? What is the place of election in the entirety of the counsel of God? To be able to ascertain this, we must necessarily consider the counsel of God in general, be it only in passing. God's counsel in this broad sense is the eternal thought and will of God concerning all created things, man and angels, moon and stars, the animate and the inanimate creation.

This decree or this counsel of God is eternal, since there was never a beginning of the thoughts of God in regard to creation. Those thoughts are as eternal as God Himself. And that counsel of God is all inclusive. From before the foundation of the world, all things were with Him in His divine thoughts, not only as He made them in the beginning, but also as they should develop throughout history. God has from before the foundation of the world decreed in His eternal counsel how things will be eternally. He determined the end of all things from the beginning. God determined how He would create all things in the beginning with a view to the consummation of all things. Creation is planned with a view to re-creation, generation to regeneration, the beginning with a view to the end. Not only this, but with a view to that end God the Lord planned the course of events, so that all in its mutual working and development must work together to attain His eternal purpose. Let us never forget that God's works are a unity, and that every creature is organically related to every other creature. Everything is planned with a view to everything else. God has therefore so determined everything in His counsel that the end of all things must be the realization of that which He had purposed in Himself.

Therefore nothing can be excluded from this counsel. Rain and drought, fruitful and unfruitful years, health and sickness, war and peace, yea, the animals of the field and the sparrows of the housetops must serve that purpose and end which God has determined in Himself. In this connection notice that this also includes the evil things: sin, pain, death, and all that is related to them. Never may we conceive of God's counsel as if it allows for adjustments, or for events not included in it. On the contrary, God decided the end, and He sovereignly determined the way and the means that should lead to that end, sin and death included.

Already at this point in our discussion we may establish that God's goal, which He determined in Himself, is that all the works of His hands must show forth His praise to the fullest extent, and must witness of the magnificence of His name. The Lord has indeed made all things for His own sake, even the wicked unto the day of evil (Prov. 16:4); for He is God and He alone, and He does all His good pleasure.

But now the question arises: How did God conceive of this end of all things to which all things in His counsel are directed? What will that unity of all things be, that consummation of all things, through which God's name will be most fully glorified and His virtues most gloriously revealed? Note that the question should be put in this way. The question is frequently asked: In what manner is God glorified in the individual works of His hands? But not enough attention is given to the relation of these works one to another.

Let us take again the example of a work of art. Naturally, I can stand in front of a beautiful building and focus my attention on the individual parts of the building. I can note the beautiful stones, the colored windows, the lofty vaults, the pointed arches, and whatever else there may be. If one architect has planned it all, then I can, in pointing out the separate parts, praise the ability of the architect. This also can be done with the works of God. This is in fact the method that is usually employed.

Now it is true that God is glorified in the wonderful, omnipotent work which He has established in the beginning. The heavens declare the glory of God and the firmament showeth forth His handiwork, and the entire creation speaks of His eternal power and godhead. With wisdom the Lord hath made it all. So, too, I can speak of the work of salvation, and, as subdivisions of this, speak separately of His gracious election and of His just reprobation. Thus I can praise God for the revelation of His sovereign love in election, and at the same time say that in reprobation He reveals His justice and wrath as well as His great power.

Yet, you immediately feel that we may not leave it at that. There was in that building, if the architect really was capable, one principal idea, and, with a view to that, all the other parts are determined. If I attend only to the parts, the result is twofold. In the first place, I have not grasped the principal idea of the whole, in which the marvelous realization of the idea is brought out. Secondly, I have not done justice to the parts, for the simple reason that I have not shown their place and purpose in relation to the whole. Thus it is with God's works. God is one. His work is one. One magnificent idea governs all. If I wish, therefore, to glorify God in His work, I must attend not only to the parts, but first to the whole, and then show how each part is related to that whole.

In regard to reprobation, for example, I can say that God sovereignly predestined some to destruction in order to glorify Himself; but if I say no more, I will have presented God as a tyrant who destroys creatures for the sole purpose of glorifying Himself. And one will say to himself: "This is a hard saying, who can hear it?" O, surely, God is sovereign; and He does with His own what He wills and no one can say, "What doest thou?" But that does not take away the thought that repeatedly arises in our hearts, Why has the all-wise God done this? Therefore we must place ourselves before the question: What is the goal, the consummation? What is the outcome? What has God determined in Himself? What is the end of all the works of His hands?

Then we must take as our starting point what we read in Ephesians 1:9, 10: "Having made known unto us the mystery of his will, according to his good pleasure which he hath purposed in himself: that in the dispensation of the fulness of times he might gather together in one all things in Christ, both which are in heaven, and which are on earth; even in him."

We cannot now give a complete explanation of this beautiful and comprehensive passage. Let it suffice that we treat the chief teachings of the text in as far as this is necessary for the treatment of our subject. First of all, it is clear that the apostle here reveals to us what God the Lord has purposed in Himself in His counsel with respect to the eternal purpose of all His works. There can be no doubt that the text deals with the eternal good pleasure of God. He has purposed in Himself from before the foundation of the world how things should be in their consummation. Hardly can it be denied that the apostle speaks of all things, the whole creation, the fullness of all that God has made. He says emphatically *all things,* both those in heaven and those on earth. I know that this has been explained as if it referred to the militant and triumphant church. Yet this conflicts with the plain meaning of the word. Here the discussion is in regard to all things. We may thus take this to mean: What has God, from before the foundation of the world, determined in Himself with respect to this present creation? What shall its consummation be?

We answer first of all that, according to the text, the entire creation shall be an intimately related and harmonious unity. Indeed all the creatures which are in heaven and on the earth shall be brought together under one head, so that all creation shall form a perfect unity. This was not the case in the beginning. There was then not one head of the entire creation. There was an earthly and a heavenly creation. Certainly, the earthly creation was united under its earthly head. Adam was king and head. But this kingship did not include the things which are in heaven; for Adam, as he stood in the first paradise, was made a little lower than the angels. Even this kingship, however, was devastated by sin. Adam fell. He broke the covenant, separating himself along with the earthly creation from the God of the covenant. The creatures now are mutually parted and separated. It is now man against man, people against people, plant against plant, animal against animal. The animal world is mutually divided, as well as separated from man. The harmony in the earthly creation is broken. Some such division also took place in heaven amongst the angels of God. But this passage of the apostle teaches us that it was God's purpose from before the foundation of the world to unite all things again into a higher and all-inclusive unity, both the things in heaven and the things on earth.

In the second place, we answer, in the light of the text, that God had determined in Himself so to unite all things that they are governed by *Christ* as King. Christ must become the Head of the new creation. Adam may not be that head. This includes that the ruling principle of the new creation shall be that Christ is Lord over all. All creation has its harmonious unity in Him. As far as Christ is exalted above Adam, so far will the future creation shine forth in blazing glory above the present creation. This not only means that all creatures shall be gathered together and united in perfect unity under the one head, Christ, but also that creation shall then be most intimately united with God. For, indeed, Christ is Immanuel, God with us, the Word that became flesh. In Him are the divine and human natures, Creator and creature in closest union, one with the other. In Christ, God joins Himself most intimately with us through the bond of the covenant. And in Christ God's tabernacle will be spread over us; and through us all things will be included in this tabernacle of God. The glorified creation shall eternally lie close to God's heart in Christ Jesus.

Thus considered, the counsel of predestination (more specifically, election, with its necessary complement, reprobation) is the heart of God's decree. This counsel of predestination determines the place which God's rational creatures, both angels and men, shall assume in this eternal unity of all things. And amongst the rational creatures, man who was made in the image of God, and whose nature was assumed by Christ, occupies the chief place. When all the works of God shall have reached their consummation, then man, in Christ Jesus, will be in closest communion and live in most intimate fellowship with God. For this reason it is impossible to place the decree of predestination on the same line with the decree of providence. Both form a unity, but so that predestination assumes the pivotal place around which all the rest revolves, and in which all finds its unity, according to the all-wise counsel of God. And this unity is formed in such a way that the decree of election assumes the chief place in predestination, not only in the sense that election is the positive side and reprobation the negative side, but also thus that reprobation serves election.

We shall enlarge upon this presently. However, this can now already be said, that since it was God's determination in the fulness of time to unite and to gather all things in Christ Jesus, it stands to reason that God's main concern is not with that which falls eternally outside of that glorified creation. When one constructs a building, his chief concern is not the stones which never find a place in the completed structure, even though they were formed as stones. Thus it is in God's counsel. Election is and remains the main purpose, to which reprobation is subordinate, whatever purpose it may serve.

So conceived, election is that part of God's counsel in which He, from before the foundation of the world, has determined which individuals will have a glorious place in the final unity of all things. Election may be defined as God's appointment of individuals to the glory of the new and everlasting creation. Election is indeed discriminating. It implies that God has chosen some in distinction from others. Nevertheless it is chiefly predestination. And, therefore, election in this connection is to be defined as that decree of God by which He sovereignly and freely, out of pure grace, without respect to merits, chose to give some a place with Christ in eternal glory. The primary purpose is the glorification of God. The motive is deepest love. He desired to glorify His children with a glory which they could never have attained in the first Adam.

Moreover, election is personal. God has known His own by name from eternity. But election is to be thought of organically. For, although election deals with individuals and is personal, yet it is also true that the elect form a unity in Christ, a glorious inheritance of God in which each has his own place. The elect constitute the body of Christ, in which each member is chosen to a certain personal destination, to his own place in the body.

Election and Reprobation

Now we are prepared to give an answer to the question, What is the place of reprobation in that scheme? God has reprobated as well as chosen. Taken by itself, reprobation is the decree of God in which He has determined, as sovereignly as in election, that some individuals should not enter eternal glory, but are destined for destruction. Thus it should be expressed. I realize it seems milder to say that God decided to leave others in their sins and ruin. This is the way it is formulated in our Canons, in which the Synod of Dordt adopted the infra standpoint, contrary to the wishes and protestations of Gomarus.

Yet, as a matter of fact, this is not a milder way of expressing it. We may close our eyes to the problem and refuse to seek an answer, but the problem remains. The question inevitably arises, How did these people fall into the sin in which God permitted them to lie? Another question also arises, Why did God leave them in this sin and misery when He could have saved them? I fully realize that all questions cannot possibly be answered. Nevertheless, it is also true that by closing our eyes to the problems that arise we fail to find a solution.

Besides, Scripture certainly teaches more. The Potter does with the clay as He pleases, and no one can deny Him the right to form of one lump of clay a vessel unto honor and of another a vessel unto dishonor. Surely, here we are taught more than that God permits something to lie where it has fallen. The vessels unto dishonor are also made by Him in accordance with His appointment. Therefore, we would rather say that reprobation is that decree of God by which He sovereignly destined some to destruction. For, certainly, the condemnation shall be on the basis of the sin and guilt of the reprobate, but never as if this reprobation rests on foreseen sin. Reprobation, even as election, is entirely, sovereignly free.

At present, however, we are not so much concerned about reprobation as such, but rather about its relation to election. The question is, What is the relation of the former to the latter? Or rather, the more weighty question, Why did God reprobate? You say: To the glorification of His name. Correct. We agree. God the Lord has wrought all things for His own sake, even the wicked to the day of evil. We grant that. But the question arises: Is God the Lord glorified to a greater extent by having reprobated some, rather than if He had saved all? Granted that the damnation of the reprobate glorifies Him eternally, would His honor not have been greater if He had saved all? Again you say, No, because then His righteous indignation would never have been revealed. But is that true? We agree, of course, that in the destruction of the reprobate God reveals His righteous anger and is thereby glorified. Was that anger not sufficiently revealed in the suffering of Christ?

Every time the same question confronts us: Why has God reprobated some? To find an answer to this we must place ourselves before the question: What is the relation of election to reprobation? Do these form a dualism? Then there is dualism in God also; then God is a God of highest love, and at the same time of deepest hatred. This surely is impossible. God does not desire the destruction of the reprobate in the same way in which He delights in the salvation and glory of His chosen people. Therefore we maintain that Scripture gives the following in answer to this very important question: Reprobation exists in order that election may be realized; reprobation is necessary to bring the chosen to the glory which God in His infinite love has appointed for them.

God loved His people with an infinite love. In His great love He determined to lead them to the glory He had appointed for them in Christ. If He determined to attain this greatest glory and lead the elect into it, it was necessary for Him, reverently speaking, to reprobate some. Not because all could not find a place in that glory, for then the question would arise, Why did God decree to create more people than could assume a place in the organism of the body of Christ? But because those who are presently to be damned must for a time serve the salvation of the elect, be it in an antithetical manner. In this sense, reprobation is a divine necessity. In this sense, the reprobate exist for the sake of the elect. They are in a certain sense the price, the ransom, which God pays for the higher glory of His children.

Of course, you will ask if we can prove this. We think we can. In the first place, we wish to refer you to the fact that this idea is not strange to God's general revelation in nature and in history. You find it proved in the life of the nations and of people in particular. On many monuments erected in honor of our soldiers who lost their lives on the battlefield, you may read the inscription, "They gave their lives that we might live." Here is a figure of election and reprobation as we are now considering it. How often it occurs that thousands lose their lives on the battlefield in order that others may live. They do not merely give their lives, but it is required of them. They were reprobated that the nation might live.

It is no different in the lives of individuals, or individual persons and animals. The mother gives life to her child, not infrequently at the expense of her own. It is virtually always true that one generation lives and dies to make room for the next. There are species of animals in which the male dies after mating. The male is cast off (reprobated) to give life to the young.

According to the Scriptures, it is no different in the plant kingdom. When a farmer sows seed in his field, he sows much more than he needs. When the seed falls into the earth and dies, there appear not only the kernels of wheat, for which the seed was planted, but also the stem, the straw, and even the chaff. Without the stem and the chaff the grain could never have germinated and ripened. The stem and the chaff serve the grain, the seed. Yet both will presently be burned by fire in order that the grain may be gathered into the barn. Here also we find election and reprobation, and in such a way that the latter serves the former, and is necessary to it.

Yet this is not all. Not only do you find a figure of this truth in the general revelation of God, but it is also literally proved in Scripture, both in various texts and in the historical accounts. The Lord declares in Isaiah 43:4 to Israel, "Since thou wast precious in my sight, thou hast been honourable, and I have loved thee: therefore will I give men for thee, and people for thy life." It is true that this passage refers to that which the Lord did for Israel in the past. But it is also true that this passage refers to the eternal counsel of God's good pleasure. For indeed God has loved His people from eternity. In His counsel they are precious in His eyes. Thus the text refers to the eternal love of God. In that eternal love He has desired to glorify and magnify His people, and to lead them to the highest possible glory in His eternal inheritance. The text says that, in order to accomplish this, God has given other people in the place of His chosen people. Because He loved His people, those others had to pay for Israel's salvation with their own lives. Israel's history proves this time and time again. Pharaoh and his host perish. They must serve Israel temporarily, but God does not hesitate to give people for the life of His people. When Israel enters Canaan, people are again given in the place of Israel. This is effectuated by the sins of these people. They have filled the measure of iniquity at the time when Israel must enter into the rest and are destroyed to make room for Israel. So it is throughout the history of Israel. Babylon also serves a purpose, namely, to chastise Jerusalem. Yet, hereby it makes itself ripe for judgment. And when it has served to realize God's counsel, Babylon is destroyed.

Thus it is literally presented in Proverbs 11:8: "The righteous is delivered out of trouble and the wicked cometh in his stead." The idea here is that the ungodly serve to deliver the righteous out of trouble, to glorify them. And having done so they perish for their sins. Still stronger is the language of Proverbs 21:18: "The wicked shall be a ransom for the righteous, and the transgressor for the upright." Here again we have the idea that God gives the wicked as a ransom, which He pays to glorify the righteous.

Naturally, this does not detract from the other truth that in reprobation God also reveals His righteousness, and is glorified in revealing His holy name. Indeed, these reprobate do not serve the salvation of the elect willingly, but as godless, and in spite of themselves. For this reason, they become guilty in serving this purpose, and are worthy of condemnation. Thus, in serving God's purpose they become ripe for destruction. Just as chaff ripens for destruction while it serves the grain, so the godless become ripe for perdition while they serve the elect.

More evident this is in the case of our Savior Himself. Surely for the glorification of the elect, the blood of the Savior must flow. But if this blood is to flow, there must be a wicked and reprobate world to shed it. There must be a Judas who betrays Him; there must be a Sanhedrin that condemns Him; there must be a mighty and godless Roman power that finally brings Him to the cross. In all this, the reprobate serve for the glorification of the elect. Without that ungodly world, the cross cannot be imagined. But the situation is also thus that the world, in crucifying the Savior, through which it serves for the glorification of the elect, becomes ripe for destruction.

As it was then, so it is now. So it will be to the end of the world. And when the end shall come, the ungodly shall be righteously condemned and damned, in sin having served God's counsel. The elect shall be eternally glorified with the Savior in the inheritance of the saints. Thus we conclude that in the unity of God's plan, reprobation necessarily serves election. God's love toward His people reigns supreme in His counsel. To reveal and to realize this love fully He brings into existence people who must finally be damned. Reprobation is the necessary antithetical counterpart of election.

Reprobation in the Preaching

On this basis we can determine the place of reprobation in the preaching of the Gospel, and, for that matter, its place in every presentation of the truth. Surely reprobation must be preached. This follows from the very fact that God has revealed it, and the complete counsel of God must certainly be preached. We can understand this necessity. Without the preaching of reprobation, not only can election, its counterpart, not be preached, but neither can justice be done to God's electing love. God's great love must always be our chief concern. That love is manifested in this that He has given His only begotten Son, that whosoever believeth in Him shall not perish, but have everlasting life. However, this becomes still more glorious if we understand that to realize this love, God has given people in the stead of His people, and given the wicked as a ransom for the righteous.

Secondly, it surely must become evident in the preaching that God is sovereign, also when a part which He first formed falls away. When we see a farmer pull out the little plants which he had previously planted, it seems sad and foolish to us, until we understand that this has its purpose. So too it is with the work of God. Unless we consider the matter from God's viewpoint, and unless we are enlightened by His wise counsel, the world's history seems a great pity, a great misery. For, although God is the ultimate Victor and will finally glorify His people, the fact remains that many creatures which He had first formed are eternally lost through the wiles of the devil and the powers of death and sin. Not so, if we present reprobation in the proper light. Then God remains sovereign. There is then no accident. Whatever God does is well done, for He does all things in wisdom.

We must not surrender an inch of ground to the idea that God wills to save all, some of which are nevertheless lost. God's counsel shall stand, and He shall remain sovereign - sovereign in regard to eternal life, and at the same time sovereign in regard to eternal perdition. Therefore reprobation must be preached; for God must remain sovereign even over the kingdom of darkness. Reprobation must be preached to the congregation from the viewpoint of election. The believers must understand that salvation is not of him that runneth, nor of him that willeth, but of God that sheweth mercy. According to God's good pleasure they have received a place in the consummation of all things. This means so much more to us when we understand that God could also sovereignly have reprobated us. There can be no question that reprobation should be preached, if one wishes to divide the Word of truth properly.

Thus, it has become evident how reprobation should be preached, and what place it should be given in the preaching of the gospel. In the first place, it has become evident that we must not have sermonettes devoted to reprobation. This is also true of election. This is true of every aspect of the truth. He who occasionally preaches only on election, without relating it whatsoever to reprobation, is not preaching election. This is still more true of reprobation, which is the antithetical counterpart of election. It belongs with election. It can be understood only in the light of election. It must accordingly be presented in its relation to election.

It is also evident that, when preaching on election and reprobation, we must not place them dualistically over against each other. They are not on the same level. They are not corresponding halves of the same thing, but together they form a unity. Reprobation should always be presented as subordinate to election, as serving the latter according to God's counsel. From this it follows that reprobation should not be preached with a certain delight in the doctrine. He who is forever preaching reprobation shows not only that he is harsh and cruel, but also that he has not understood the work of the Lord God. God's love remains the central thought. He has chosen in His eternal love; and, for the sake of this love, He has also reprobated. Thus all God's work becomes a beautiful organic unity. In this way He is and remains God, and He alone. Thus, at the conclusion of all this, we exclaim in adoration with the apostle, "Oh, the depth of the riches both of the wisdom and knowledge of God; for of him and through him and to him are all things! To him be glory forever!"

God will presently make all things new. Then He will fully reveal His everlasting and glorious Kingdom to all His children. Then the kingdom of Christ, including His chosen church, will be inseparably united with God. And it will appear that this divine and beautiful work is so marvelous and so glorious that not only was it doubly worth all the suffering of this present time, but also it is costly enough to give people as a ransom for it. The glory of the Lord shall, through Jesus Christ, shine forth with heavenly radiance over all the works of His hands, forever!

Also available on Amazon

(Available in *Kindle & Paperback*)

Also available on Amazon

(Available in *Kindle & Paperback*)

Also available on Amazon

(Available in *Kindle & Paperback*)

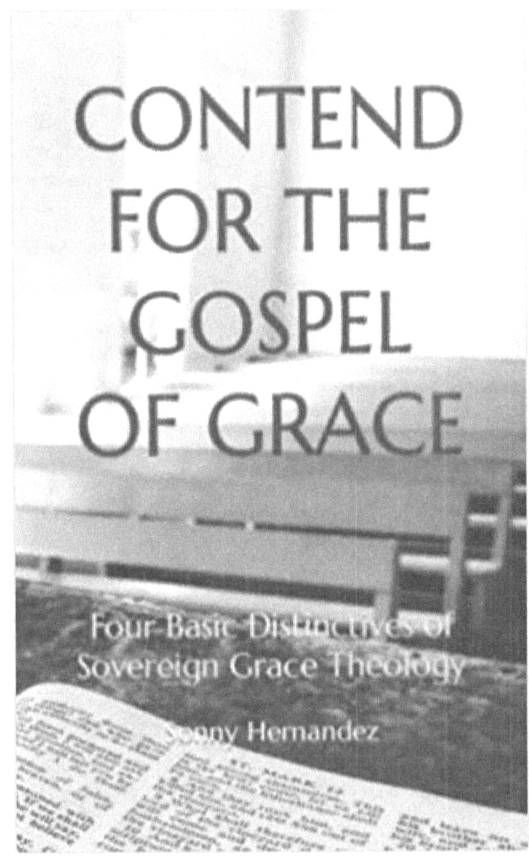

Also available on Amazon

(Available in *Kindle & Paperback*)

ABOUT THE AUTHOR

Sonny Hernandez is pastor of Trinity Gospel Church (KY), and he served 20+ years in the armed forces. He earned a doctorate in pastoral theology/leadership from Tennessee Temple University. He served as an adjunct professor for McKendree University (Radcliff, KY Campus) and Grand Canyon University (distance learning). Sonny has authored several books, and has written several published articles for news sources and journals.

TrinityGospelChurchKY.com

ἡ χάρις τοῦ κυρίου Ἰησοῦ Χριστοῦ καὶ ἡ
ἀγάπη τοῦ θεοῦ καὶ ἡ κοινωνία τοῦ
ἁγίου πνεύματος μετὰ πάντων ὑμῶν